CHALLENGING LIFESTYLE

SERIES 1

NICKY GUMBEL

First published 2008

ISBN 13: 978 1 905887 27 9

Published by Alpha International
Holy Trinity Brompton, Brompton Road, London SW7 1JA
Email: publications@alpha.org
Design by James Vincent

CONTENTS

page

Blessed are the poor in spirit, for theirs is the kingdom of heaven.

Blessed are those who mourn, for they will be comforted.

Blessed are the meek, for they will inherit the earth.

Blessed are those who hunger and thirst for righteousness, for they will be filled.

MATTHEW 5:3-6

how to find the **secret** of **happiness**

TALK **.01**

INTRODUCTION

Blessed: (Greek) *makarios*
'blessed, fortunate, happy – the privileged recipient of God's favour.'

Are we looking for happiness in the wrong places?

Happiness is **not dependent** of our outward condition.

Jesus' teaching is counter-cultural.

“When you first read the Sermon on the Mount, you think "Its impossible". Then, when you read it again, you think "Nothing else is possible".”

G.K Chesterton

1 BLESSED ARE THE POOR IN SPIRIT, FOR THEIRS IS THE KINGDOM OF HEAVEN.

True happiness comes from **being depressed.**

- Not the medical condition of being depressed, but rather being 'brought low', being 'weakened'
- Jesus uses the language of paradox

Becoming a Christian can lead to growing spiritual dissatisfaction.

We fall short of God's standards, and become 'beggars'.

- The kingdom of heaven flings open its doors to beggars
- The kingdom starts with a desperate need for God

2 BLESSED ARE THOSE WHO MOURN, FOR THEY WILL BE COMFORTED.

True happiness comes from **grieving**.

Jesus is not talking here about crying.

- 'Mourn' is a strong word
- Genesis 37:35 – Jacob mourns his son Joseph

Two mistaken views of Christian life:

- Christians must never be happy
  - Jesus' disciples should be absurdly happy
- Christians must never be unhappy
  - **"There is .... a time to weep"**
    ECCLESIASTES 3:1,4

Dietrich Bonhoeffer: *The Cost of Discipleship*

We should weep over:

- Sins of the world
- Our own sins

Grief drives us into God's arms.

NOTES

BLESSED ARE THE MEEK, FOR THEY WILL INHERIT THE EARTH.

True happiness comes from **being broken.**

Meek does not mean:

- Weak
- Spineless
- Feeble

But rather:

- Gentle
- Unassuming

Moses is described as `the meekest man on the whole planet'.

Submit to God.

It is liberating to say to God: `Lord, I'm willing to do whatever you want me to do.'

4 BLESSED ARE THOSE WHO HUNGER AND THIRST FOR RIGHTEOUSNESS.

True happiness comes from being **deeply dissatisfied.**

A **desperate** hunger and thirst.

Righteousness is:

- Right relationship with God
- The right relationship with everyone else that follows

Jesus says if we hunger and thirst for righteousness, we will be satisfied.

CONCLUSION

There is a progression:

- We see our desperate need
- We grieve over our need
- We give ourselves to God
- We desire a right relationship with him

When we are in a right relationship with God, we are deeply satisfied.

NOTES

DISCUSSION QUESTIONS

1. Would you describe yourself as happy?

2. What is the difference between being 'happy' and being 'blessed'? What does Jesus mean by his use of the word 'blessed'?

3. What does it mean to be 'poor in spirit'? How does this help us to find true happiness?

4. How do we deal with being unhappy as Christians? What difference can it make to know God's love in our hearts?

5. What does a right relationship with God look like? Why would that make you truly happy?

6. What difference does being part of a Christian community make to our happiness?

NOTES

Blessed are the merciful,
for they will be shown mercy.
Blessed are the pure in heart,
for they will see God.
Blessed are the peacemakers,
for they will be called sons of God.
Blessed are those who are persecuted because of righteousness, for theirs is the kingdom of heaven.

Blessed are you when people insult you, persecute you and falsely say all kinds of evil against you because of me. Rejoice and be glad, because great is your reward in heaven, for in the same way they persecuted the prophets who were before you.

You are the salt of the earth. But if the salt loses its saltiness, how can it be made salty again? It is no longer good for anything, except to be thrown out and trampled by men.

"You are the light of the world. A city on a hill cannot be hidden. Neither do people light a lamp and put it under a bowl. Instead they put it on its stand, and it gives light to everyone in the house. In the same way, let your light shine before men, that they may see your good deeds and praise your Father in heaven.

how to **change** the **world** around you

INTRODUCTION

Can we make any difference?

- Huge need
- Individual unhappiness
- Spiritual and moral vacuum

Jesus said we can change the world around us – not by *withdrawal*, but by *involvement*.

We should be salt and light in our immediate surroundings:

- In our workplace
- In our families
- In our sports teams
- With our neighbours

1 BLESSED ARE THE MERCIFUL, FOR THEY WILL BE SHOWN MERCY.

Don't give people what they 'deserve', but give them what they **don't deserve.**

The virtuous circle: we forgive because we are forgiven.

Mercy is also kindness to the:

- Hungry
- Homeless
- Sick

2 BLESSED ARE THE PURE IN HEART, FOR THEY WILL SEE GOD.

Don't put on a mask, but **be transparent**

- Integrity
- Openness
- Sincerity
- Authenticity

We must be able to talk honestly and openly, and not remove our Christian 'uniform'.

The pure in heart are the same in every situation.

The pure in heart see God.

HOW TO CHANGE THE WORLD

NOTES

3 BLESSED ARE THE PEACEMAKERS, FOR THEY WILL BE CALLED CHILDREN OF GOD.

Don't stir up conflict, but **make peace.**

“It takes a long time to make peace; a short time to make tension. Many, many people make tension; few people make peace. Wherever you find tension, you must make peace.”

Nelson Mandela

Peacemaking must start:

- In our marriages
- In our neighbourhoods
- In our churches

God is a peacemaker.

As children of God, we are called to make peace.

God loves to see his children getting on with each other.

4 BLESSED ARE THOSE WHO ARE PERSECUTED BECAUSE OF RIGHTEOUSNESS, FOR THEIRS IS THE KINGDOM OF HEAVEN.

Don't expect anything in return except **criticism.**

Righteousness sums up the previous seven Beatitudes:

- A right relationship with God
- A right relationship with others

Christianity is still a persecuted religion.

“Rejoice and be glad, because great is your reward in heaven.”

We are in line with the prophets who went before us.

CONCLUSION

We are not helpless.

These are unique Christian values:

- to be merciful
- to be pure in heart
- to be a peacemaker
- to rejoice when persecuted

They are the values that hold the world together, and they will transform the world around us.

If we follow Jesus and live our lives in the way he teaches, our lives have a purpose.

NOTES

DISCUSSION QUESTIONS

1. What sphere of influence do you have in the world? How can you take seriously your responsibility to be salt and light there?

2. What opportunities have you had recently to show 'mercy'?

3. How transparent are you? Are you consistent and authentic in every area of your life?

4. Are you good at building peace in your relationships and in the workplace?

5. How do you react to criticism? In what way can persecution be a blessing?

6. How would you like to be remembered?

7. Why is focusing on becoming more like Christ the key to transforming the world around you?

NOTES

Do not think that I have come to abolish the Law or the Prophets; I have not come to abolish them but to fulfill them.

I tell you the truth, until heaven and earth disappear, not the smallest letter, not the least stroke of a pen, will by any means disappear from the Law until everything is accomplished. Anyone who breaks one of the least of these commandments and teaches others to do the same will be called least in the kingdom of heaven, but whoever practices and teaches these commands will be called great in the kingdom of heaven.

For I tell you that unless your righteousness surpasses that of the Pharisees and the teachers of the law, you will certainly not enter the kingdom of heaven.

how to **understand** the old testament

TALK .03

INTRODUCTION

Authority of the Old Testament.

“Do not think I have come to abolish the Law or the Prophets; I have not come to abolish them...”
MATTHEW 5:17

Interpretation of the Old Testament.

“...I have come... to fulfil them.”
MATTHEW 5:17

1 GET TO KNOW THE PERSON

Jesus fulfils God's story **MATTHEW 1:1-17**.

Three equal periods:

- Abraham – David, 14 'generations' (800 years)
- David – exile, 14 'generations' (400 years)
- Exile – Jesus, 14 'generations' (600 years)

1. Read the Old Testament to understand Jesus.
2. Read the Old Testament through the lens of Jesus.

2 ENJOY THE PROMISES

Jesus fulfills God's promise

MATTHEW 1:18-4:14

- There are over 300 prophecies in the Old Testament about Jesus
- 29 prophecies were fulfilled in a single day

“...no matter how many promises God has made, they are "yes" in Christ Jesus.”

2 CORINTHIANS 1:20

Sometimes the reality far exceeds the literal fulfillment.

THE OLD TESTAMENT

NOTES

3 LIVE IT OUT IN PRACTICE

Jesus fulfils God's law **MATTHEW 5-7**

1. Study Jesus' teaching to see what it really means.
2. Look at Jesus' life to see how it should be lived.
3. Experience the results of Jesus' death and resurrection in order to live it out in practice.

A righteousness is revealed apart from the law –

a righteousness that comes through faith in Jesus Christ.

He gives us the Holy Spirit so that we can live out this righteous life in practice.

THE OLD TESTAMENT

CONCLUSION

Marcian was wrong: Jesus did not reject the Old Testament; he endorsed it.

"It is written..." **MATTHEW 4**

- Jesus quotes Deuteronomy

"...Christ is the key to the central contents of the Old Testament, but at the same time it is the Old Testament which provides the clue to Christ."

G.E. Wright

"...the Holy Spirit inspired Scripture. And now, each time we open this book, Scripture breathes the Holy Spirit. Reading the Scriptures without the Holy Spirit would be like opening a book in the dark."

Father Raniero Cantalamessa

THE HOLY SPIRIT POINTS US TO JESUS. WHEN WE READ THE BIBLE, WE ENCOUNTER JESUS.

NOTES

DISCUSSION QUESTIONS

1. What is your view of the Old Testament and your experience of reading it?

2. What is Jesus' attitude to the Old Testament? Are we surprised by it? Does it challenge our own attitude?

3. How can we get to know the person of Jesus better through the Old Testament?

4. What does it mean to read the Old Testament 'through the lens of Jesus'?

5. Discuss some of God's promises in the Old Testament that you think Jesus fulfills. What difference does this make to your understanding of the Old Testament? Discuss the implications of 2 Corinthians 1:20.

6. In what ways does Jesus 'fulfill' Old Testament law? How do these apply to your life?

NOTES

You have heard that it was said to the people long ago, 'Do not murder, and anyone who murders will be subject to judgment.' But I tell you that anyone who is angry with his brother will be subject to judgment. Again, anyone who says to his brother, 'Raca,' is answerable to the Sanhedrin. But anyone who says, 'You fool!' will be in danger of the fire of hell.

"Therefore, if you are offering your gift at the altar and there remember that your brother has something against you, leave your gift there in front of the altar. First go and be reconciled to your brother; then come and offer your gift.

"Settle matters quickly with your adversary who is taking you to court. Do it while you are still with him on the way, or he may hand you over to the judge, and the judge may hand you over to the officer, and you may be thrown into prison. I tell you the truth, you will not get out until you have paid the last penny.

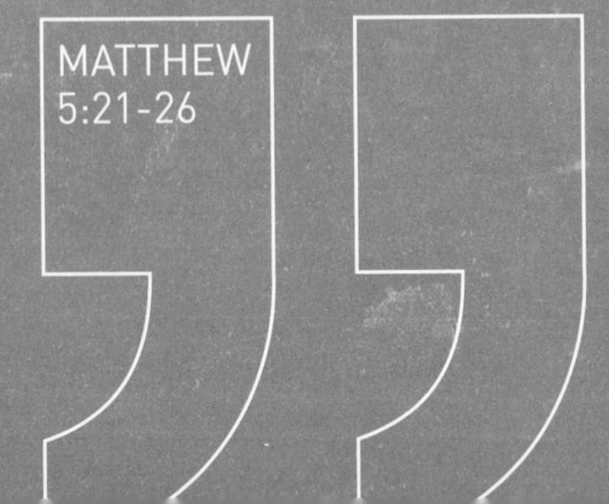

how to handle
anger

INTRODUCTION

Four different categories of expressing anger at work (Rick Warren):

- Maniacs
- Mutes
- Martyrs
- Manipulators

Anger is an emotion, and a natural passion.

Physically, anger causes changes in our bodies.

1 CONSIDER THE CAUSE

God himself gets angry.

- Righteous vs unrighteous
- Rational vs irrational
- Constructive vs destructive
- Love of others vs love of self

The anger of Jesus was always based on his love of others.

2 PRESS THE PAUSE BUTTON

God is "...slow to anger..." **PSALM 145:8**

"A fool is quick tempered." **PROVERBS 14:17**

Pressing the pause button gives us:

- time to reflect
- time to talk to other people about it

ANGER

NOTES

3 WATCH THE WORDS

“...anyone who says to a brother or sister, ‘Raca’, is answerable to the Sanhedrin. But anyone who says, ‘You fool!’ will be in danger of the fire of hell.”

MATTHEW 5:22B

Words are very powerful, and they can be very damaging.

There is nothing wrong with loving confrontation:

- Children need discipline in a loving way
- Disagreements need to be brought into the open
- Personal growth involves being able to listen to criticism

Jesus isn’t suggesting we suppress our feelings, but rather he is warning against reacting out of anger.

4 MASTER THE MIND

“You have heard that it was said to the people long ago, ‘Do not murder, and anyone who murders will be subject to judgment.’ But I tell you anyone who is angry with a brother or sister will be subject to judgment’.”

MATTHEW 5:21-22A

Jesus did not contradict Moses, but rather drew attention to the true interpretation of Moses.

We must win the battle in our minds.

NOTES

5 COUNT THE COST

"Do not let the sun go down while you are still angry, and do not give the devil a foothold."

EPHESIANS 4:26-27

Jesus says that anger sometimes leads to:

- destruction of families, relationships, marriages
- abuse of children
- violent crime
- breakdown of communities

If left unchecked, anger can lead to sudden destruction.

ANGER

6 PURSUE THE PEACE

"...go and be reconciled to them..."

MATTHEW 5:22B

Jesus warned against divisions both inside and outside the church.

"Settle matters quickly with your adversary who is taking you to court."

MATTHEW 5:25

"A lean settlement is worth more than a fat lawsuit."

Charles Haddon Spurgeon

Where possible, we must seek reconciliation within the Christian community.

"Therefore, if you are offering your gift at the altar and there remember that your brother has something against you, leave your gift there in front of the altar. First go and be reconciled to your brother; then come and offer your gift."

MATTHEW 5:23-24

CONCLUSION

We all fall short, but we can be different – we can be an alternative society.

It is possible to be different through:

- the power of the cross
- the blood of Christ
- the power of the Resurrection

> **“FORGIVENESS IS NOT AN EMOTION... FORGIVENESS IS AN ACT OF THE WILL.”**
>
> *Corrie Ten Boom*

DISCUSSION QUESTIONS

1. Which one of the four categories of expressing anger that Rick Warren identifies [maniacs, mutes, martyrs, manipulators] do you associate with most?

2. What in your life causes anger most often?

3. Do you think Jesus' call to another way is unrealistic in today's increasingly stressful and fragmented world or a standard worth aiming for?

4. Is there ever a time when anger is justified?

5. How often do you allow time to pass before getting angry in a situation? What practical ways have you found helpful in 'pressing the pause button'?

6. Do the words you use change depending on the scenario? Is it possible to only ever speak words of love?

7. How do our minds affect the decisions we make when we're angry? How can we best control our minds?

8. What is the cost of unrestrained, uncontrolled anger? What have been some of the consequences in your own life?

9. When is there a time for anger and a time for peace and reconciliation? What marks those times? How has God guided you in the past in those situations?

NOTES

You have heard that it was said, 'Do not commit adultery.'

But I tell you that anyone who looks at a woman lustfully has already committed adultery with her in his heart.

If your right eye causes you to sin, gouge it out and throw it away. It is better for you to lose one part of your body than for your whole body to be thrown into hell.

And if your right hand causes you to sin, cut it off and throw it away. It is better for you to lose one part of your body than for your whole body to go into hell.

MATTHEW
5:27-30

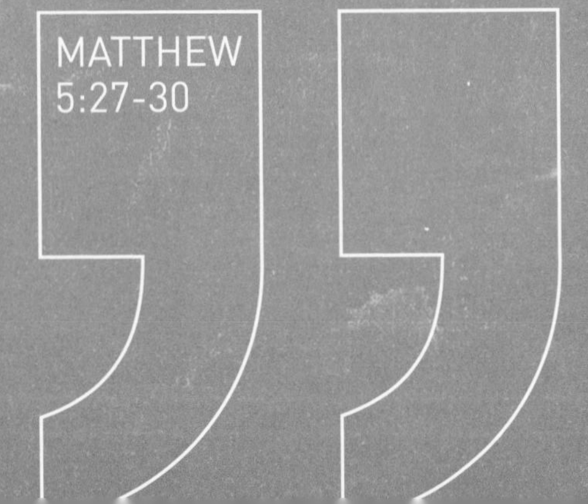

how to approach **sex** in the 21st century

TALK .05

INTRODUCTION

Biblical framework:

Creation: Sex is **good**

Fall: Sex is **complicated**

Redemption: Sex can be **restored**

Glorification: Sex is **not an end in itself**

1 BE RADICAL

Being a Christian is counter-cultural.

"You have heard that it was said. But I tell you..."

MATTHEW 5:27, 28

The command is not just limited to the physical act of adultery; it's about the heart.

Our culture is moving in the opposite direction to Jesus' teaching:

- Sex outside of marriage is now regarded as the norm
- Pornography has become mainstream
- The physical act of adultery has become far more acceptable

It takes courage to swim against the tide.

2 BE ROMANTIC

"...for this reason a man will leave his father and mother and be united to his wife, and the two will become one flesh. So they are no longer two, but one. Therefore what God has joined together, let no-one separate."

MATTHEW 19:5-6

In the context of marriage, sex

- signifies
- seals
- and then brings about an unbreakable, total, personal unity

Without such a commitment, sex is cheapened; it is a life-uniting act without a life-uniting intention.

"Human beings are highly complex, and the soul is infinitely deep... if you're mingling your soul with another soul, there's no end to the depth of both your souls."

Rob Bell

NOTES

3 BE REPENTANT

"...anyone who looks... lustfully has already committed adultery..."

MATTHEW 5:28

- We all fall short of God's standards
- It's never too late to start again
- The word repentance is a positive word in the Bible

SEX

4 BE RUTHLESS

"If your right eye causes you to sin, gouge it out and throw it away. It is better for you to lose one part of your body than for your whole body to be thrown into hell. And if your right hand causes you to sin, cut it off and throw it away. It is better for you to lose one part of your body than for your whole body to go into hell."

MATTHEW 5:29-30

- Jesus doesn't mean a literal, physical self-maiming, but rather a ruthless, moral self-denial.
- He wasn't forbidding looking at someone, but rather looking lustfully at someone.
- It's not the thoughts that are sinful; rather, it's the entertaining of them.

Adultery destroys something very precious and therefore we must avoid it at all costs – starting not with the act, but with the heart.

NOTES

5 BE ROLE MODELS

"... you are the salt of the earth."
MATTHEW 5:13

"... you are the light of the world."
MATTHEW 5:14

We must be different in a positive way.

We are to be a society of deep, intimate friendships and relationships.

All of us, whether married or single, are to be role models to the world.

CONCLUSION

We all have a drive within us that is a gift from God.

Epithymia (the word Jesus uses for lust here) can have a positive sense: it can refer to a desire to be with Christ.

"Life is not about toning down and repressing your God given energy; it's about channeling it and focusing it and turning it loose on something beautiful, something pure and true and good..."

Rob Bell

TO CHANNEL WHAT GOD HAS GIVEN US WE NEED TO BE FILLED WITH THE HOLY SPIRIT, AND WE NEED TO SEEK GOD FIRST.

NOTES

DISCUSSION QUESTIONS

1. What is your view of sex? How do you respond to each of the following:
   - Creation: sex is good
   - Fall: sex is complicated
   - Redemption: sex can be restored
   - Glorification: sex is not an end in itself

2. What do you think our culture's view of sex is?

3. How can we be radically counter-cultural in handling sex as Christians?

4. How can we deal with the pressures of our culture to conform in the sexual arena?

5. Jesus sets the bar very high in this area (Matthew 5:28). Why do you think this is? Take time to talk about repentance and receiving God's love and forgiveness.

6. How can we put Matthew 5:29-30 into practice? How can we guard our hearts in this area?

7. How can being part of a Christian community help us to be role models when it comes to sex?

NOTES

"It has been said, 'Anyone who divorces his wife must give her a certificate of divorce.'

But I tell you that anyone who divorces his wife, except for marital unfaithfulness, causes her to become an adulteress, and anyone who marries the divorced woman commits adultery."

'Some Pharisees came to him to test him. They asked, "Is it lawful for a man to divorce his wife for any and every reason?"

"Haven't you read," he replied, "that at the beginning the Creator 'made them male and female,' and said, 'For this reason a man will leave his father and mother and be united to his wife, and the two will become one flesh'? So they are no longer two, but one. Therefore what God has joined together, let man not separate."

"Why then," they asked, "did Moses command that a man give his wife a certificate of divorce and send her away?"

Jesus replied, "Moses permitted you to divorce your wives because your hearts were hard. But it was not this way from the beginning. I tell you that anyone who divorces his wife, except for marital unfaithfulness, and marries another woman commits adultery."

The disciples said to him, "If this is the situation between a husband and wife, it is better not to marry."'

Jesus replied, "Not everyone can accept this word, but only those to whom it has been given. For some are eunuchs because they were born that way; others were made that way by men; and others have renounced marriage because of the kingdom of heaven. The one who can accept this should accept it."

MATTHEW 5:31-32
MATTHEW 19:8-12

how to respond to divorce

TALK .05

INTRODUCTION

People can be affected by divorce:

- Directly
- Indirectly

All of us are affected because we belong to a society that is deeply affected by this issue.

We are now living in an increasingly fatherless generation.

Jesus responded to questions about divorce by talking about marriage.

1 CHOOSE WISELY

Celibacy:

"...and others have renounced marriage because of the kingdom of heaven."
MATTHEW 19:12

Marriage:

"Haven't you read," he replied, "that at the beginning the Creator 'made them male and female,' and said, 'For this reason a man will leave his father and mother and be united to his wife, and the two will become one flesh'? So they are no longer two, but one. Therefore what God has joined together, let no-one separate."
MATTHEW 19:4-6

Before you are married, you are free to choose anybody. The moment you get married, the time to choose is over.

When choosing a marriage partner, we must:

- Take risks
- Allow for trial and error
- Avoid being over-intense

2 INVEST MASSIVELY

"So they are no longer two, but one. Therefore what God has joined together, let no-one separate."
MATTHEW 19:6

Jesus' model for marriage is the best and most beautiful.

"Never mention divorce... Never joke about it. Rule it out from the start."
Bishop Sandy Millar

- Marriage is not easy, but we must invest massively
- We must make our marriage relationship our priority, above our work and our children

Nicky and Sila Lee: The Marriage Book.

Put Jesus at the centre of your marriage.

We can invest in our parents' marriage; in our children's marriages; in our friends' marriages.

NOTES

3 CONCEDE RELUCTANTLY

Moses did not **command** that a man must give his wife a certificate of divorce, but rather he **permitted** it.

Background to this debate: Shammai vs Hillel.

Our view of divorce must be consistent with the broader context of Jesus' teaching.

- Jesus and the rest of the New Testament confirm that marriage is permanent, and that divorce should only be allowed in the most extreme cases.
- We must do everything in our power to avoid divorce and to bring about reconciliation but, as a last resort, we have to concede reluctantly.

4 REBUILD CAREFULLY

Even in the society of Jesus' day, it was generally assumed that divorced people **would** remarry.

It might be that God calls a person to witness to the permanence of marriage by **not** remarrying.

There must always be repentance, and attempts at reconciliation.

We must find a balance between:

- Jesus' prophetic statements **(marriage is for life)**
- His pastoral teaching **(divorce does happen).**

There is no perfect solution, but a service of blessing can be the best way to balance the prophetic and the pastoral.

DIVORCE

NOTES

EMBRACE UNCONDITIONALLY

We must beware of judging people.

- Divorce involves unimaginable pain.

“He has sent me to bind up the broken-hearted”
ISAIAH 61:1, QUOTED BY JESUS IN LUKE 4:18

“The Lord is close to the broken hearted and saves those who are crushed in spirit.”
PSALM 34:18

The ministry of Jesus is:

- grace
- forgiveness
- transformation

We must give people **hope** again.

CONCLUSIO

The church needs to stress the:

- permanence of marriage
- possibility of reconciliation
- difference that Jesus makes

NOTES

DISCUSSION QUESTIONS

1. Discuss the impact of divorce on those affected directly, indirectly and on society in general.

2. What can help us to choose wisely when it comes to getting married?

3. At the moment you get married 'the moment for choosing is over'. Is this helpful?

4. What attitudes and approaches to marriage help us to sustain marriage and avoid divorce?

5. Under what circumstances might divorce be permissible? As well as Matthew 5:32 see also 1 Corinthians 7:15.

6. How can we balance the prophetic with the pastoral in the area of remarriage in church?

7. How can we support and encourage those who are broken hearted in this area?

NOTES